Animals Are Amazing 2:

More Fun Facts for Kids

written by J.R. Ellis

Animals Are Amazing

Animals have found amazing ways to survive in every environment on Earth!

Some build homes in trees, underground, or even in the ocean. Others withstand extreme temperatures, from the icy Arctic to the scorching desert, using special adaptations to stay hot or cold. Some animals move in unusual ways—slithering, hopping, or gliding—while others are built for speed or use slow movements to stay hidden. Some travel long distances through migration, following food or the seasons. Communication is key in the animal kingdom—creatures use sounds, scents, and even body movements to send messages. Life thrives underwater, in the sky with animals that fly, and in the dark, where nocturnal animalsexplore the world at night. Sadly, some species are endangered, struggling to survive due to habitat loss and other threats.

By learning how animals live, move, and communicate, we can help protect these incredible creatures for the future!

Did you know?

Lionfish are striking with their striped bodies and long, flowing fins—but they're also venomous predators! Native to the Indo-Pacific, these fish use their fan-like fins to corner prey and strike with lightning speed. Their spines deliver a painful sting to predators, making them nearly untouchable. Invasive in parts of the Atlantic and Caribbean, lionfish have few natural enemies and can upset local ecosystems. Despite their beauty, lionfish are a powerful reminder that looks can be deceiving in the animal kingdom!

Did you know?

Squirrels are clever problem-solvers with incredible physical abilities. They can leap over 10 feet and twist their bodies midair to land safely, even after long falls! Their sharp claws and rotating ankles help them race up and down trees with ease. In clever experiments, squirrels can complete obstacle courses, outsmart traps, and learn patterns to earn food rewards. They're also excellent planners, hiding hundreds of nuts and remembering where they buried them months later!

Animal Homes

Just like people, animals need a safe and comfortable place to live. Animal homes come in all shapes and sizes! Some birds make nests from twigs and leaves, while others find cozy spots in trees or bushed. Some animals dig burrows in the ground for shelter, and others find caves or logs to rest in. Each animal picks or builds an amazing home that is just right for them, helping protect them from bad weather and keeping them safe from predators. These homes are important for animals to feel secure!

Clownfish

Clownfish live among the stinging tentacles of sea anemones, creating a safe and protective home. Unlike other fish, they have a special coating on their skin that prevents them from getting stung. In return, clownfish help keep the anemone clean, forming a unique partnership that benefits them both.

Badger

Badgers dig burrows called setts, which have many tunnels and chambers, creating a safe underground home. These provide shelter from predators and harsh weather. Some badger families live in the same sett for generations, expanding and maintaining their tunnels to keep their homes comfortable.

Puffin

Puffins dig burrows into cliffs or hillsides to create safe, hidden nests. These underground homes protect their chicks from predators and harsh weather, keeping them warm and secure. Puffins use their strong beaks and webbed feet to dig tunnels, sometimes over three feet deep! Inside, they line their nests with grass and feathers for extra comfort. These cozy burrows provide the perfect shelter until the chicks are ready to head out to sea.

Hermit Crab

Hermit crabs don't build their own homes—they find old seashells to live in! Their soft bodies need protection, so as they grow, they search for larger shells. Sometimes, they even line up and trade shells in a carefully timed exchange!

Grizzly Bear

Grizzly bears are powerful animals that dig dens in the ground to hibernate through the winter. Using their strong claws, they create sheltered burrows in hillsides, under tree roots, or even in caves. Inside, they stay warm and survive by living off the fat they stored during the warmer months. Mother grizzlies give birth while hibernating, keeping their tiny cubs safe inside the den until spring, when they finally emerge to explore the world.

Hot and Cold

Animals have amazing ways of keeping warm in the cold or cool in the heat! In very hot places, animals have adapted to survive with little water and lots of heat. Some use special features, like flapping their ears to cool off or storing water in their bodies. In cold regions, animals stay warm by using thick fur or layers of fat. They might huddle together for warmth or have special coats to protect them from the snow and ice. Whether in the hottest deserts or surrounded by ice and snow, animals are built to live comfortably in their environments!

Hippopotamus

Hippos spend most of their day in rivers and lakes to stay cool under the hot African sun. Their thick skin dries out quickly, so they secrete an oily substance that acts like sunscreen. Even though they seem slow, hippos can run surprisingly fast on land when defending themselves!

Moose

Moose are built for the freezing winters of Canada and Alaska. Their thick fur keeps them warm, and their long legs help them move through deep snow. In winter, they eat twigs and bark when food is scarce and use their powerful antlers to clear snow and fend off predators.

African Elephant

African elephants thrive in the hot savannas, using their giant ears like fans to stay cool. Their wrinkled skin helps trap moisture, and they cover themselves in mud to protect against the sun and insects. These powerful animals use their long tusks to dig for food and water, break branches, and defend themselves. Elephants also rely on their trunks for drinking, spraying water, and communicating with their herd through touch and sound.

Polar Bear

Polar bears live in the freezing Arctic, where their thick fur and a layer of blubber keep them warm in icy waters and freezing winds. Their white fur helps them blend into the snow and ice, making it easier to sneak up on seals while staying hidden from predators like orcas.

Camel

Camels are built for life in the desert, where temperatures soar and water is scarce. They can go for days without drinking, surviving on the fat stored in their humps. Their thick eyelashes shield their eyes, and they can close their nostrils to keep out blowing sand. Wide, padded feet help them walk on hot, shifting sand, and they also conserve water by producing dry waste and sweating very little, making them perfectly adapted to extreme desert conditions.

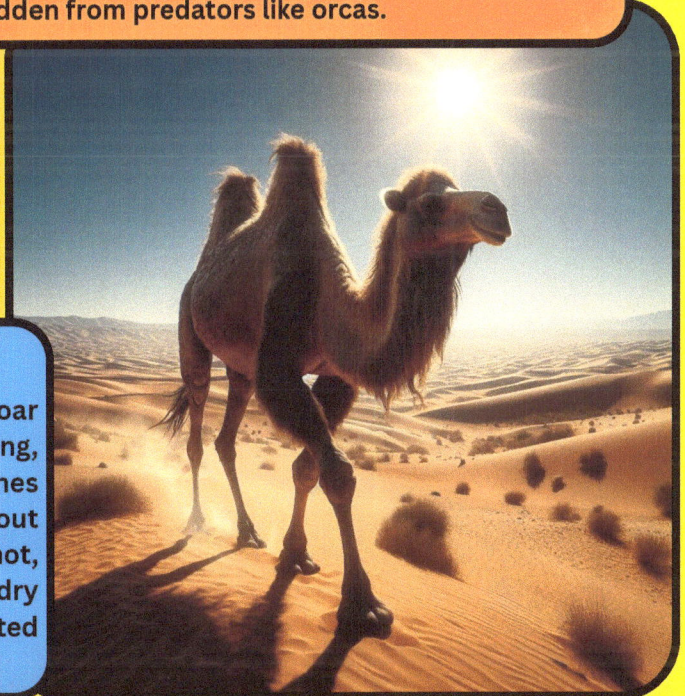

Did you know?

Emperor penguins are the tallest and heaviest penguins in the world—and they're built for survival! These amazing birds can dive over 1,800 feet deep and stay underwater for more than 20 minutes, all while searching for fish in icy Antarctic waters. Unlike most birds, emperor penguins don't build nests. Instead, the father balances the egg on his feet and covers it with a warm flap of skin called a brood pouch. While the moms hunt for food, the dads huddle together in freezing winds to keep their eggs safe and warm!

Did you know?

The *okapi* looks like a mix between a zebra and a giraffe—but it's actually the giraffe's closest living relative! Found in the dense rainforests of the Congo, okapis have velvety brown fur with white striped legs that help them blend into the shadows of the forest. Their long, purple tongues can reach over 12 inches and are so flexible they can clean their own ears!

The *giant squid* is one of the ocean's most mysterious and elusive creatures! Growing up to 40 feet long, with eyes the size of basketballs, it's one of the largest invertebrates on Earth. Its long arms and tentacles are covered in powerful suction cups lined with sharp hooks, helping it catch prey in the dark ocean depths. Giant squids live thousands of feet below the surface. Despite their size, they're still no match for their greatest predator—the sperm whale, which bears scars from their fierce underwater battles.

The *star-nosed mole* has one of the strangest noses in the animal kingdom! Its snout is covered with pink, fleshy tentacles that form a star shape—and those tentacles are superpowered sensors. This mole uses its nose to detect and identify prey in less than a tenth of a second, making it the fastest-eating mammal on Earth! Living in wet, marshy soil, it's also an excellent swimmer. It can even smell underwater by blowing bubbles and re-sniffing them!

How Animals Move

Animals have different ways of getting around, each suited to their needs! Some animals walk or run on legs, while others slither on the ground or hop to get where they're going. Birds use their wings to fly high in the sky, and fish swim gracefully through the water with their fins. Whether they run, swim, hop, or crawl, each animal has an amazing way of moving that helps them thrive in their environment, find food, escape danger, or travel to new places.

Kangaroo

Kangaroos hop on their powerful hind legs, using their long tails for balance as they move across the Australian outback. Their strong legs allow them to leap great distances—sometimes over 25 feet in a single bound! When standing still, they use their tails like a tripod to stay steady and support their weight.

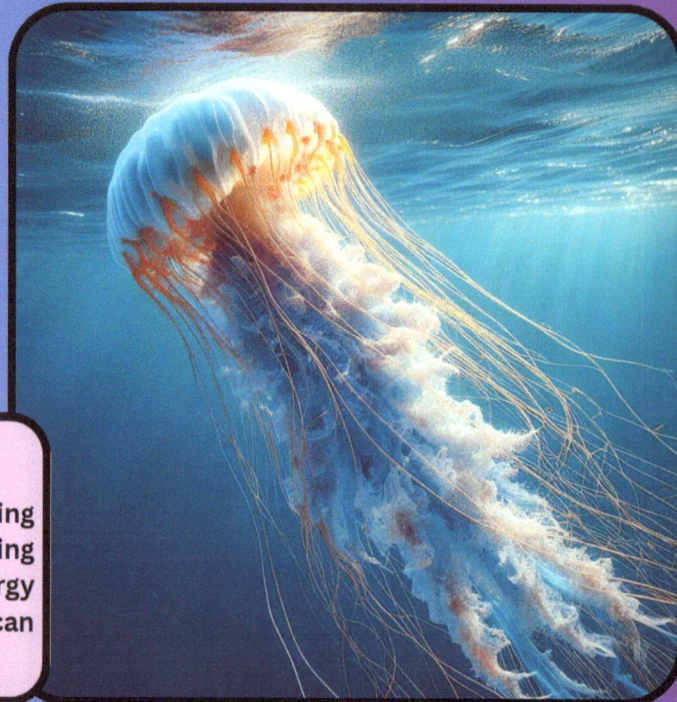

Jellyfish

Jellyfish move by pulsing their bell-shaped bodies, pushing water behind them to glide forward. This gentle, flowing motion helps them drift with ocean currents, using little energy as they travel. While they seem to float aimlessly, they can pulse faster when needed to catch prey or avoid danger.

Crab

Crabs move in a unique way—scuttling sideways instead of walking forward! Their strong, jointed legs are built for speed, helping them escape quickly when danger is near. This sideways movement allows them to fit through tight spaces and stay balanced on uneven surfaces like rocky shores and sandy beaches. Some species of crabs can even swim by using special back legs shaped like paddles, making them excellent movers both on land and in water!

Iguana

Iguanas are expert climbers, using their sharp claws to grip tree branches near rivers and lakes. If threatened, they can leap from trees into the water and swim to safety, using their powerful tails to propel themselves through the currents.

Ostrich

Ostriches are the fastest birds on land, capable of sprinting up to 43 miles per hour! Their long, powerful legs help them escape predators like lions and cheetahs across the African plains. With each stride covering over 10 feet, they can maintain high speeds for long distances. If threatened, an ostrich can also deliver a powerful kick with sharp claws, making them not only fast runners but also fierce defenders

Fast and Slow

In the animal world, speed can make a big difference when it comes to survival! Some animals are incredibly fast, allowing them to catch their food or escape from danger. Speedy creatures, like certain fish and birds, can zoom through the water or dive at amazing speeds to find their meals. However, being slow has its advantages too—animals like sloths and tortoises move steadily, conserving energy and blending into their surroundings. Whether they are speedy hunters or slow movers, animals have adapted their speed to fit their lifestyles and needs in the wild.

Cheetah

Cheetahs are the fastest land animals, capable of sprinting up to 60 miles per hour in short bursts. Their long legs, flexible spines, and lightweight bodies help them accelerate quickly. Using their tails for balance, they make sharp turns while chasing prey, making them amazing hunters on the open plains.

Sloth

Sloths move slowly, using their long limbs and curved claws to hang from tree branches. Their sluggish pace helps them blend into the treetops, making it harder for predators to spot them. Moving slowly also conserves energy, allowing them to survive on their low-nutrient diet of leaves.

Peregrine Falcon

Peregrine falcons are the fastest birds, diving at speeds over 200 miles per hour to catch prey in mid-air! Even in normal flight, they can reach 40 to 60 mph. Their speed comes from powerful flight muscles, stiff feathers, and pointed wings built for precision. They often live on cliffs or tall buildings, using high altitudes to gain momentum before striking. With their unmatched speed and accuracy, peregrine falcons are expert aerial hunters.

Black Marlin

Black marlins are the fastest fish in the ocean, reaching speeds of 82 miles per hour! Their sleek, torpedo-shaped bodies and crescent tails help them glide through the water. These speedy hunters chase fish, squid, and octopus while using their speed to escape predators.

Giant Tortoise

Giant tortoises are incredibly slow, moving at just 0.16 miles per hour! But their slow pace isn't a problem—it is exactly what they need. Walking so slow helps them to conserve energy. With their tough, domed shells protecting them from predators, they don't need to move fast to stay safe. These gentle giants can live over 100 years, spending their long lives grazing on plants, basking in the sun, and slowly exploring their island or grassland homes.

Did you know?

Cockroaches might not be anyone's favorite houseguest, but they're true survival experts! These ancient insects have been around for over 300 million years—since before the dinosaurs. They can survive a whole week without their heads and hold their breath for up to 40 minutes! Some species can go a month without food, and they're incredibly fast—running up to 3 miles per hour. As gross as they may seem, cockroaches are built to last—and they're one of nature's most unstoppable survivors.

Did you know?

The *bobcat* may look like a giant housecat, but it's a stealthy wild hunter built for survival! Named for its short "bobbed" tail, this powerful feline is found all across North America—from forests and deserts to swamps and mountains. Bobcats are mostly solitary and can leap up to 12 feet to catch prey like rabbits, birds, and even deer! Their tufted ears help them hear the tiniest sounds, and their spotted fur blends into the shadows. Though elusive, bobcats play a key role in nature by keeping small animal populations in balance.

Did you know?

The *roadrunner* isn't just a cartoon character—it's a real bird that can sprint faster than most humans! Found in the deserts and scrublands of the American Southwest, this speedy bird can run up to 20 miles per hour. Roadrunners rarely fly, preferring to dash after lizards, snakes, insects, and even small birds. They use their long tails for balance as they zigzag through the brush. One of the most surprising facts? Roadrunners can kill and eat venomous rattlesnakes by striking them with their beak!

Did you know?

Hedgehogs are tiny insect-eating mammals covered in thousands of sharp spines! When frightened, they roll into a tight little ball, using their spines as armor to protect their soft belly. These nocturnal foragers have an excellent sense of smell and hearing, and they love to snack on bugs, worms, and even small frogs. Despite their prickly look, hedgehogs are surprisingly gentle and shy creatures.

Migration

Some animals are great travelers, making amazing journeys each year! Migration is when animals travel long distances to find food, better weather, or safe places to have their young. Many birds fly thousands of miles to warmer homes in the winter, while some mammals swim across oceans to reach their feeding grounds. By migrating on these long trips, animals adapt to changing seasons and find what they need to survive and thrive throughout the year.

Humpback Whale

Humpback whales migrate thousands of miles each year, traveling between cold polar waters, where they feed, and warm tropical seas, where they mate and give birth. These long journeys help protect their calves, giving them a safe place to grow before returning to rich feeding grounds.

Arctic Tern

Arctic terns make the longest migration of any animal, flying nearly 24,000 miles each year from the Arctic to Antarctica and back. They follow the summer sun, staying in warm climates and enjoying more daylight than any other creature on Earth as they travel between polar regions.

American Bison

American bison roam the plains in massive herds, migrating with the seasons to find fresh grass. These powerful animals travel great distances, following ancient paths used for generations. Their movement helps shape the landscape, as their hooves churn the soil, encouraging new plant growth. By staying together in large numbers, bison protect themselves from predators and ensure their herd always has access to food in the vast open grasslands.

Canada Goose

Canada geese migrate in large flocks, flying in a familiar V-formation to conserve energy on long journeys. Their honking calls signal the changing seasons as they travel between Canada and the U.S., though some flocks have changed routes due to shifting habitats and food sources.

Sockeye Salmon

Sockeye salmon make an incredible journey, swimming from the ocean back to the rivers where they were born to lay their eggs. They can travel up to 900 miles upstream, leaping over rapids and waterfalls to reach their birthplace. Young salmon hatch in freshwater, spend years growing there, then migrate to the ocean. After maturing, they return to freshwater to spawn, completing their life cycle before dying within weeks.

Animal Communication

While humans use five senses—sight, hearing, smell, taste, and touch—some animals have super special senses that help them explore the world in amazing ways. Some can use sound waves to see in the dark, while others sense tiny electric signals from far away. There are animals that detect vibrations in the ground or use their sense of smell to find food from miles away. These unique skills let animals sense things beyond what humans can see or hear, making them fantastic at surviving and thriving in their environments.

Dolphin

Dolphins are highly intelligent and use clicks, whistles, and squeaks to communicate. Each dolphin has a unique whistle, like a name, to recognize friends and family. They also use echolocation, sending out sound waves and listening for echoes to navigate, hunt, and understand their underwater world.

Coyote

Coyotes communicate using a mix of howls, yips, and barks. Their eerie howls help them find pack members, while short yips signal excitement or play. Barks warn of danger, and some calls even trick rivals into thinking more coyotes are nearby, helping them defend their territory.

Hyena

Hyenas are highly social animals that live in clans and use many ways to communicate. Their famous 'laughs' signal excitement or nervousness, while whoops help them call to clan members from miles away. Grunts and growls warn others of danger, and scent marking helps define territory. Hyenas also use body language, like raised tails for dominance or lowered heads for submission, making their communication just as complex as their strong social bonds.

Bullfrog

Bullfrogs have deep, loud croaks that can be heard from far away. Males croak to attract mates and warn other frogs to stay out of their territory. Each bullfrog has a unique voice, and their calls can even help scientists tell them apart!

Cricket

Crickets make their signature chirping sound by rubbing their wings together. Males chirp to attract mates, and the louder and faster the chirp, the better their chances. Some crickets also use chirps to defend territory or warn rivals to stay away. Interestingly, crickets chirp more often in warm weather, and scientists can even estimate the temperature based on how many chirps they hear in a minute!

Did you know?

Tarantulas may look scary, but they're actually shy and gentle giants of the spider world! These hairy arachnids can grow as big as a dinner plate, yet their bite is rarely dangerous to humans. Tarantulas have poor eyesight but rely on sensitive hairs on their legs to detect vibrations in the ground—helping them hunt insects, small lizards, and even frogs! When threatened, some tarantulas kick tiny itchy hairs off their abdomen to irritate predators. Amazingly, some tarantulas can live up to 30 years in the wild!

Did you know?

Ibex are wild mountain goats known for their amazing climbing skills! These sure-footed animals can scale steep cliffs and narrow ledges that would terrify most other creatures. Their split hooves have rubbery pads that grip rocky surfaces like climbing shoes. Ibex live in high-altitude habitats where predators can't easily follow. Males grow long, curved horns that can reach over three feet and are used in dramatic head-butting battles during mating season.

Piranhas are small but powerful fish known for their razor-sharp teeth and strong jaws. Despite their scary reputation, most piranhas are scavengers or only eat plants and insects. However, when food is scarce, they may feed in frenzied groups, stripping prey quickly with their sharp, interlocking teeth. Piranhas live in South American rivers. Their keen senses help them detect blood in the water from far away, making them efficient—even if misunderstood—hunters of the river.

Did you know?

Deer are gentle, graceful animals known for their speed and agility. A mother deer, called a doe, gives birth to one or two spotted fawns each spring. These white spots help fawns blend into the forest floor, keeping them safe from predators. For the first few weeks, fawns stay hidden and still while their mother forages nearby. Even though they seem fragile, fawns can stand within hours of birth and run surprisingly fast after just a few days!

Life Underwater

Beneath the surface of oceans, lakes, and rivers lies an amazing world of animals that thrive in water. Many creatures are perfect for swimming with their fins and gills, while others need to come to the surface for air. There are many kinds of animals that live in water all around the world - including fish, mammals, amphibians, reptiles, and crustaceans. Some animals move gracefully through the water, while others drift with the currents. From bright coral reefs and deep ocean depths to quiet lakes and winding rivers, the underwater world is an amazing place full of life where animals thrive!

Octopus

Octopus are masters of disguise, changing their color and skin texture to match their surroundings. They live on the ocean floor and can squeeze into tiny cracks and crevices to hide. With their eight arms and clever brains, they're among the most intelligent invertebrates in the sea.

Catfish

Catfish live in rivers and lakes, where they search for food along the bottom. They're easy to recognize by their whisker-like barbels, which help them feel and taste their surroundings. These special sensors make it easier to hunt in dark or muddy water where other fish might struggle.

Bull Shark

Bull sharks are powerful swimmers that can live in both saltwater and freshwater. They've been found far upriver and even in lakes! This unique ability helps them travel long distances. Bull sharks are strong, adaptable, and one of the few shark species that thrive in a wide range of habitats.

Leopard Seal

Leopard seals are fierce Antarctic predators known for their spotted coats and powerful jaws. They hunt penguins, fish, and other seals. Despite their size, they swim fast and silently beneath the ice, surprising prey with stealth and speed.

Sea Turtle

Sea turtles live in warm ocean waters and can hold their breath for hours while swimming. They surface to breathe and return to sandy beaches to lay eggs. Hatchlings must race to the sea to survive. With strong flippers and streamlined shells, sea turtles glide gracefully through the water, traveling thousands of miles during their lifetime.

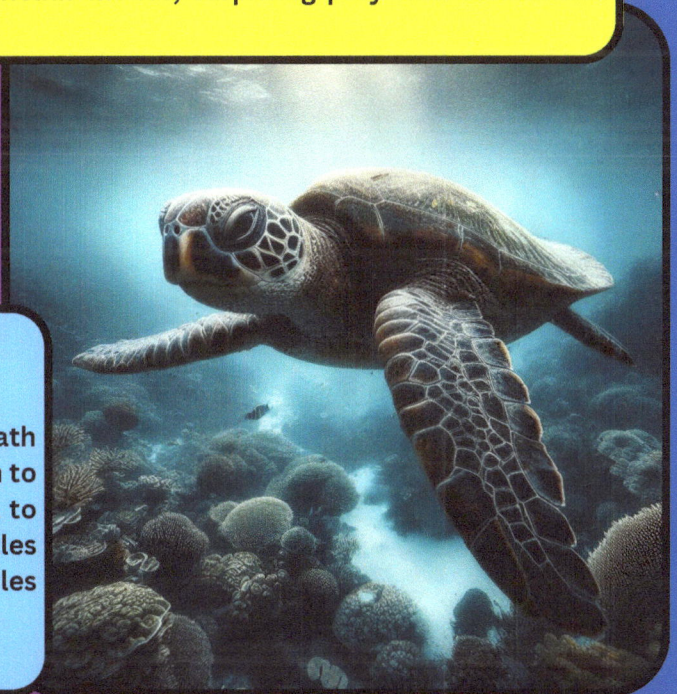

Animals That Fly

Did you know that some animals are amazing problem-solvers, using their smarts and creativity to survive in the wild? Many clever animals have learned to use tools, like sticks or rocks, to help them find food, build homes, or defend themselves. But it doesn't stop there—some animals show amazing problem-solving skills in other ways! They solve puzzles, work together in teams, or come up with clever tricks to outsmart predators or catch their next meal. Whether it's using objects to get what they need or finding creative solutions to challenges, these smart creatures show that animals can be very resourceful.

Flying Fish

Flying fish escape danger by leaping out of the water and gliding through the air! Their long fins act like wings, letting them soar above the surface for up to 650 feet. This clever trick helps them avoid fast predators like tuna, marlin, and dolphins.

Bat

Bats are the only mammals that can truly fly. They use echolocation—sending out high-pitched sounds and listening for echoes—to hunt insects in the dark. Some bats eat fruit or nectar, helping pollinate plants. Despite spooky stories, bats play an important role in keeping ecosystems healthy.

Hummingbird

Hummingbirds are tiny, colorful birds with wings that beat up to 80 times per second! They can hover in place, fly backwards, and even upside down. These amazing fliers feed on nectar and help pollinate flowers as they go. Their fast heartbeats and speedy metabolism mean they're always on the move, searching for energy-rich food.

Bumblebee

Bumblebees are fuzzy, buzzing insects that play a big role in pollinating flowers. They flap their wings incredibly fast, creating a strong vibration that helps release pollen. Without bumblebees, many plants—and our food—wouldn't grow as well.

Swan

Swans are graceful water birds known for their long necks, powerful wings, and strong pair bonds. They glide across lakes with elegance but can be fiercely protective of their young. Swans often mate for life, forming loyal partnerships. Their nests are large and built near water, where they care for their cygnets until they're ready to swim.

Did you know?

Blue jays are clever birds known for their bold personalities and loud calls. They store acorns and other nuts to eat later, often remembering dozens of hiding spots. In fact, they help forests grow by forgetting a few of those buried seeds. Blue jays are also known for their family loyalty—mated pairs stay together year-round and share parenting duties. Young jays may even stick around to help raise the next group of chicks. With their striking colors and sharp minds, these birds are much more than just noisy neighbors!

Did you know?

Water buffalo love to wallow in muddy ponds and rivers—not just to stay cool, but to protect their skin from bugs and sunburn! These powerful animals have been helping farmers for thousands of years, pulling plows and carts across Asia. Their wide hooves help them walk through soggy, swampy ground without sinking. Despite their size, water buffalo are surprisingly gentle and social, living in herds with strong bonds.

Did you know?

Wolverines are small but incredibly strong and fearless animals, often called "the little bears of the north." They live in cold, rugged places and have thick fur that keeps them warm even in the harshest winters. With powerful jaws and sharp claws, they can take down animals much larger than themselves —or scavenge from other predators. Wolverines have large feet that act like snowshoes, helping them move easily through deep snow.

Did you know?

Starfish, also called sea stars, aren't actually fish at all! They have no bones, no brain, and no blood—but they're full of surprises. Starfish can regenerate lost arms, and some species can regrow an entire body from just one arm! Instead of swimming, they move slowly using hundreds of tiny tube feet on their underside. These feet also help them pry open clams and oysters, their favorite meals.

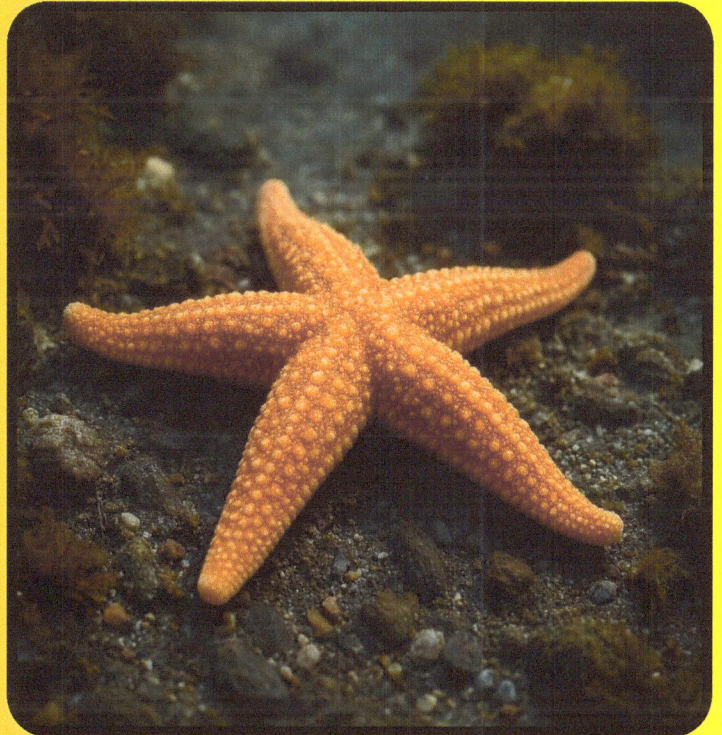

Nocturnal Animals

Did you know some animals sleep during the day and wake up at night? Nocturnal animals are amazing because they come alive when it's dark, using their special senses to see and hear better in the night. They explore under the stars, looking for food and having adventures. These animals are great at living in the dark, helping them find meals and stay safe from animals that are awake during the day.

Raccoon

Raccoons are nocturnal foragers with excellent night vision. They use their sensitive hands to explore and feel for food in the dark. They have great night vision, which helps them find snacks like berries and bugs in the dark.

Owl

Owls are nighttime hunters with amazing eyesight and incredible hearing. Their wings are built for silent flight, letting them glide quietly through the dark. With sharp eyes, keen ears, and powerful talons, owls catch small animals like mice, even in total darkness. They are masters of stealth and surprise.

Sugar Glider

Sugar gliders are tiny, tree-dwelling marsupials that can glide through the air! Using the stretchy skin between their arms and legs, they soar from branch to branch like furry parachutes. These nocturnal creatures love sweet foods like nectar and fruit. They live in social groups and communicate with chirps, clicks, and squeaks, staying close to their gliding buddies.

Gecko

Geckos are small lizards with amazing climbing skills. Their feet have tiny hairs that grip walls and ceilings, even glass! Some geckos can drop their tails to escape danger and grow them back later. They're active mostly at night.

Tasmanian Devil

Tasmanian devils are small, fierce marsupials found only in Tasmania. They have strong jaws that can crush bones, and they often eat every part of their prey. Devils make loud screeches and growls when feeding or defending territory. Though once common, their numbers have dropped due to disease, making conservation efforts important for their survival.

Endangered Animals

Many animals live and work together in groups to help each other thrive! By teaming up, animals can share tasks, find food more easily, and protect one another from dangers. Some animals form large groups to stay safe from predators, while others work together to build homes or raise their young. Whether they are hunting, gathering food, or keeping warm, working as a team makes these animals stronger and more successful in their environment. Teamwork is an amazing survival strategy that helps animals stay safe and happy!

Giant Panda

Giant pandas are gentle animals known for their striking black-and-white fur and their love of bamboo - they can eat up to 40 pounds every day . Once critically endangered, they've become a symbol of wildlife conservation. Thanks to protected habitats and breeding programs, their numbers are slowly growing—but they still need our help to survive in the wild.

Mountain Gorilla

Mountain gorillas live in misty forests and are powerful yet gentle giants. They share about 98% of our DNA and live in close-knit family groups. Once on the brink of extinction, their numbers are growing thanks to conservation efforts—but they remain endangered and need continued protection to survive.

Red Panda

Red pandas are shy, tree-dwelling animals with fluffy tails and reddish fur. They spend most of their time in trees, munching on bamboo and fruit. Though they look like raccoons or bears, they belong to their own unique family. Red pandas are endangered due to habitat loss, but conservation efforts are helping protect these charming, acrobatic creatures.

Axolotl

Axolotls are unusual salamanders that stay in the water their whole lives. They have frilly gills and big smiles. They can regrow lost limbs, even parts of their heart or brain! Found in Mexico, axolotls are rare and need protection to survive.

Orangutan

Orangutans are intelligent apes that live in the rainforests of Borneo and Sumatra. They build nests in trees and use tools to find food. With long arms and strong hands, they swing gracefully through the forest. Orangutans are endangered due to habitat loss, but conservation efforts are working to protect these gentle, thoughtful creatures and their forest homes.

For Bryce and Jack

ISBN: 978-1-969494-04-8

www.ingramcontent.com/pod-product-compliance
Lightning Source LLC
Chambersburg PA
CBHW060854270326
41934CB00002B/132